GODALMING

RONALD HEAD is a life member of the Friends of Godalming Museum. He has written four books on Godalming (Godalming in Old Picture Postcards, Volumes 1-4), and as a keen amateur photographer has supplied or processed photographs for another nine local history books. Both Ron and John Young, who researched material for this book, are guides for town walks.

JOHN YOUNG, a lifelong Godalming resident, is a member of the local history society, and part-time librarian at the museum. He probably knows more about the town than anyone else.

The Old Forge, Pound Lane 1910 62243

GODALMING

RONALD E HEAD
with research by John Young

FRANCIS FRITH'S
TOWN & CITY
MEMORIES

First published as Godalming, A Photographic History of your Town
in 2001 by Black Horse Books, an imprint of The Francis Frith Collection
Revised edition published in the United Kingdom in 2005 by
The Francis Frith Collection as Godalming, Town and City Memories

Hardback limited edition 2005
ISBN 1-84589-048-5

Paperback edition 2005
ISBN 1-85937-976-1

Text and Design copyright © The Francis Frith Collection®
Photographs copyright © The Francis Frith Collection®
except where indicated

The Frith® photographs and the Frith® logo are reproduced under licence from
Heritage Photographic Resources Ltd, the owners of the Frith® archive and trademarks.
'The Francis Frith Collection', 'Francis Frith' and 'Frith' are registered trademarks of Heritage
Photographic Resources Ltd.

All rights reserved. No photograph in this publication may be sold to a third party other
than in the original form of this publication, or framed for sale to a third party.
No parts of this publication may be reproduced, stored in a retrieval system, or transmitted,
in any form, or by any means, electronic, mechanical, photocopying, recording or otherwise, without
the prior permission of the publishers and copyright holder

British Library Cataloguing in Publication Data

Godalming
Town and City Memories
Ronald E Head, with research by John Young

The Francis Frith Collection®
Frith's Barn, Teffont,
Salisbury, Wiltshire SP3 5QP
Tel: +44 (0) 1722 716 376
Email: info@francisfrith.co.uk
www.francisfrith.co.uk

Aerial photographs reproduced under licence from Simmons Aerofilms Limited
Historical Ordnance Survey maps reproduced under licence from Homecheck.co.uk

Printed and bound in England

Front Cover: **GODALMING, CHURCH STREET 1906** 57050t
The colour-tinting in this image is for illustrative purposes only,
and is not intended to be historically accurate

Every attempt has been made to contact copyright holders of illustrative material.
We will be happy to give full acknowledgement in future editions for any items not
credited. Any information should be directed to The Francis Frith Collection.

AS WITH ANY HISTORICAL DATABASE, THE FRANCIS FRITH ARCHIVE IS CONSTANTLY BEING CORRECTED AND
IMPROVED, AND THE PUBLISHERS WOULD WELCOME INFORMATION ON OMISSIONS OR INACCURACIES

Francis Frith's Town & City Memories

Contents

The Making of an Archive	6
Godalming from the Air	8
Early History	10
High Street	12
Byways and Buildings	32
Ordnance Survey Map	34
River, Road and Rail	50
Brabner Map	62
Industry	64
The Churches	70
Godalming Schools	74
Farncombe	82
Names of Pre-Publication Buyers	86

VOUCHER FOR FREE MOUNTED PRINT — 91

The Making of an Archive

Francis Frith, Victorian founder of the world-famous photographic archive, was a devout Quaker and a highly successful Victorian businessman. By 1860 he was already a multi-millionaire, having established and sold a wholesale grocery business in Liverpool. He had also made a series of pioneering photographic journeys to the Nile region. The images he returned with were the talk of London. An eminent modern historian has likened their impact on the population of the time to that on our own generation of the first photographs taken on the surface of the moon.

Frith had a passion for landscape, and was as equally inspired by the countryside of Britain as he was by the desert regions of the Nile. He resolved to set out on a new career and to use his skills with a camera. He established a business in Reigate as a specialist publisher of topographical photographs.

Frith lived in an era of immense and sometimes violent change. For the poor in the early part of Victoria's reign work was a drudge and the hours long, and ordinary people had precious little free time. Most had not travelled far beyond the boundaries of their own town or village. Mass tourism was in its infancy during the 1860s, but during the next decade the railway network and the establishment of Bank Holidays and half-Saturdays gradually made it possible for the working man and his family to enjoy holidays and to see a little more of the world. With characteristic business acumen, Francis Frith foresaw that these new tourists would enjoy having souvenirs to commemorate their days out. He began selling photo-souvenirs of seaside resorts and beauty spots, which the Victorian public pasted into treasured family albums.

Frith's aim was to photograph every town and village in Britain. For the next thirty years he travelled the country by train and by pony and trap, producing fine photographs of seaside resorts and beauty spots that were keenly bought by millions of Victorians.

The Rise of Frith & Co

Each photograph was taken with tourism in mind, the small team of Frith photographers concentrating on busy shopping streets, beaches, seafronts, picturesque lanes and villages. They also photographed buildings: the Victorian and Edwardian eras were times of huge building activity, and town halls, libraries, post offices, schools and technical colleges were springing up all over the country. They were invariably celebrated by a proud Victorian public, and photo souvenirs – visual records – published by F Frith & Co were sold in their hundreds of thousands. In addition, many new commercial buildings such as hotels, inns and pubs were photographed, often because their owners specifically commissioned Frith postcards or prints of them for re-sale or for publicity purposes.

In order to gain some understanding of the scale of Frith's business one only has to look at the catalogue issued by Frith & Co in 1886: it runs to some 670 pages. By 1890 Frith had created the greatest specialist photographic publishing company in the world, with over 2,000 stockists! The picture on the right shows the Frith & Co display board on the wall of the stockist at Ingleton in the Yorkshire Dales (left of window). Beautifully constructed with a mahogany frame and gilt inserts, it displayed a dozen scenes.

The Making of an Archive

Postcard Bonanza

The ever-popular holiday postcard we know today took many years to appear, and F Frith & Co was in the vanguard of its development. Postcards became a hugely popular means of communication and sold in their millions. Frith's company took full advantage of this boom and soon became the major publisher of photographic view postcards.

Francis Frith died in 1898 at his villa in Cannes, his great project still growing. His sons Eustace and Cyril continued their father's monumental task, expanding the number of views offered to the public and recording more and more places in Britain, as the coasts and countryside were opened up to mass travel. The archive Frith created continued in business for another seventy years. By 1970 it contained over a third of a million pictures of 7,000 cities, towns and villages. The massive photographic record Frith has left to us stands as a living monument to a special and very remarkable man.

This book shows your town as it was photographed by this world-famous archive at various periods in its development over the past 150 years. Every photograph was taken for a specific commercial purpose, which explains why the selection may not show every aspect of the town landscape. However, the photographs, compiled from one of the world's most celebrated archives, provide an important and absorbing record of your town.

From the Air

GODALMING From the Air

Godalming from the Air 1957 AFA68206

Early History

The Market House 1903
49198

This view is the one most visitors will remember. Variously called the Old Town Hall, The Market House, and the Pepperpot, this little Georgian building has come to symbolise Godalming. Standing at the junction of High Street and Church Street, it forms a fine focal point from all sides. Yet the Borough Council debated its demolition in 1897, 1908 and 1913. The printer Craddock, whose shop lay behind it, thought it damaged his trade, and campaigned vigorously for its removal. Note the old parish pump, still there (until 1880 the town had no piped water supply), and the granite setts which paved the road until 1913. The schoolboys could be from Charterhouse.

Location, the estate agents say, is everything. Certainly it must have been the location of Godalming that first led its founders to settle where the rivers Wey and Ock join and the valley floor broadens. This area of water meadows, known as the Lammas Lands, has provided grazing for cattle for centuries. The town itself was established on a dry sandy shelf above flood level. Later, the availability of streams for water power and the suitability of the surrounding hills for sheep led to growth in the production of woollen cloth on which the town's prosperity depended for centuries. Then, in the canal era, it was its situation at the head of navigation that brought trade to the town.

With the increasing importance of Portsmouth as a naval base in the 17th and 18th centuries, location as a mid-way point for an overnight stop on the coach journey from London gave a boost to the town's inns. Following the building of the railway, and especially the completion of the direct line to Portsmouth in 1859, the coaching trade died. But Godalming's proximity to pleasant countryside led in late Victorian times to an influx of people with money, who wanted homes with easy access to both town and country. In Edwardian times that same proximity brought to the area many who wanted a base for cycling expeditions at weekends, and teashops. And recently, it was the easy access to London by train that encouraged the growth

Early History

of housing areas on the town's perimeter for those who needed to commute daily to the city.

There is no evidence of Roman occupation; everything points to a Saxon beginning, perhaps as early as the 6th century. Two Saxon windows - 'occuli' - were discovered in the parish church in the 1890s. The name Godalming is Saxon: there has been speculation that it sprang from a leader, Godhelm (he of the good helmet), and his ing (meadow) or ingas (land of his people). What is certain is that in AD 880 King Alfred the Great bequeathed the manor to his nephew, Ethelwald. He rebelled against Alfred's successor, however, and was killed in battle. The manor reverted to the Crown.

The Domesday survey, in 1086, listed three mills here. Initially corn mills, they were later adapted for other uses, including use in medieval times as 'fulling' mills, for the treatment of woollen cloth. Wool cloth making was so important here that when Queen Elizabeth granted the town its Charter in 1574, a woolsack and a ram were included in the new coat of arms. However, demand for the cloth slackened in the early 17th century and much poverty followed. Relief came from the use of the newly-invented stocking knitting frame, and a cottage industry developed. Later proper 'manufactories' were established, and for much of the 19th century Godalming was a fully fledged industrial town. Other industries

THE HIGH STREET

BELOW: THE MARKET HOUSE 1903 49265

When this photo was taken the Market House was still in use for its original purpose as a Council chamber, although its inadequacy was already apparent. The ground floor was then still used as a market room. For much of the 20th century it housed a men's public convenience, and served as a waiting room for people 'intending to travel by the motor-omnibuses plying between Godalming, Guildford and other places'.

RIGHT: THE MARKET HOUSE 1935 86771

From 1908 until 1987 the Pepperpot was used to house the town's museum. The RAC man is a hint of the traffic problems current in 1935. The large half-timbered building was the former White Hart, one of the town's main coaching inns since the 16th century. It closed in 1932 - note the estate agents' board, which advertised that the two upper floors were still to let, three years later.

included the quarrying of the local sandstone ('Bargate') and leather tanning. It was in one of the leather mills that the generator was sited for the town's only real claim to international fame - it was the first place in the world to have a public electricity supply, in 1881, three weeks ahead of Chesterfield.

For many towns, the succession of Francis Frith's wonderful photographs, taken over more than half a century, record changes in the buildings, charting the course of demolition and reconstruction. In Godalming however, the record is one of continuity. The buildings in the very first photo taken of the High Street in 1854, are, with only one exception, unchanged above shopfront level today. No serious damage was done in either world war. There have of course been changes in other parts of the town, many of them, especially recently, in Bridge Street. But it is the less obvious changes, of who occupied which shop, of varying economic prosperity, and of changes in transport, that are revealed in the photos on these pages.

THE HIGH STREET

Godalming's streets have been described as 'tortuously twisting and narrow', but that is perhaps poetic licence. A better description, of the High Street at least, is 'slightly sinuous'. It runs through the centre of the town like a spine, on 'a line which has evolved rather than been designed'. The original line may have been a track first trodden over 1400 years ago.

Adequate for pedestrians and even horse-drawn vehicles, the street is certainly narrow, and was soon found woefully deficient when mass motor traffic arrived. This was part of the main road from London to Portsmouth, and with no rear access for most of the shops and no car park, congestion was soon a problem. An early expedient was to restrict parking to one side of the street on even-numbered dates and the other side on odd dates. This one-sided parking is shown clearly in photo 85497, page 24. And there were speed limits, enforced by police traps. But with Guildford's main street also difficult for motors, a by-pass for both towns was soon essential, and this was built in 1937. There is now a by-pass for the 1937 by-pass, and an inner relief road in Godalming itself.

The most prominent building in the High Street is the market house. The right to hold a market was first granted by King Edward I in 1300, and it was probably held at the west end of the High Street near its junction with Church Street, for this is where the medieval market house was built. It was on occasion rented out and was even used to house French prisoners of war overnight. By 1814 its condition was described as 'ruinous', and a public meeting was called to decide what should be done. In the event it was replaced by the present building, financed by public subscription, and known, at first derisively but now affectionately, as the Pepperpot. The ground floor was sometimes used as a market - see photo 49265, where apparently a florist is in occupation - though it must always have been very cramped. The upstairs room served as a council meeting chamber, until the great expansion in local government functions at the end of the 19th century when Farncombe was added to the Borough and fire, police, water and public health were taken on. This necessitated the building in 1908 of the council offices in Bridge Street (see photo 59949 on page 46).

A high street comprised of only shops is a fairly recent concept. The main function of the street was originally for dwellings, and some of those built in earlier times have survived, though now converted to other uses. The last High Street house used for a dwelling, The Square, was given to the Borough as recently as 1946, and used for a while as a restaurant before finding a role as a doctors' group practice. The National Westminster bank is housed in half of a 17th century house: the other half, demolished in the 60s, was well known and loved as Jones the ironmongers. Photos G23085 and 54163A, pages 20 and 18 are separated by 59 years and exemplify the continuity typical of shops in the town. Another house was that of Dr. Parsons, seen in photo G23032, page 28, which by 1965 had become the Trustee Savings Bank (photo G23109, page 27).

The High Street

The High Street

High Street 1910 62238

Looking west from the Pepperpot, this end of the High Street was once called Sand Street. The Stedman family's home is prominent in the centre; they sold wines and spirits from a shop where the porch is now. On the extreme left is Withers, corn merchants, whose Hatch Mill was close by. The enamel sign on the chimney for Keen & Sons, bakers, (disappeared only recently).

The High Street

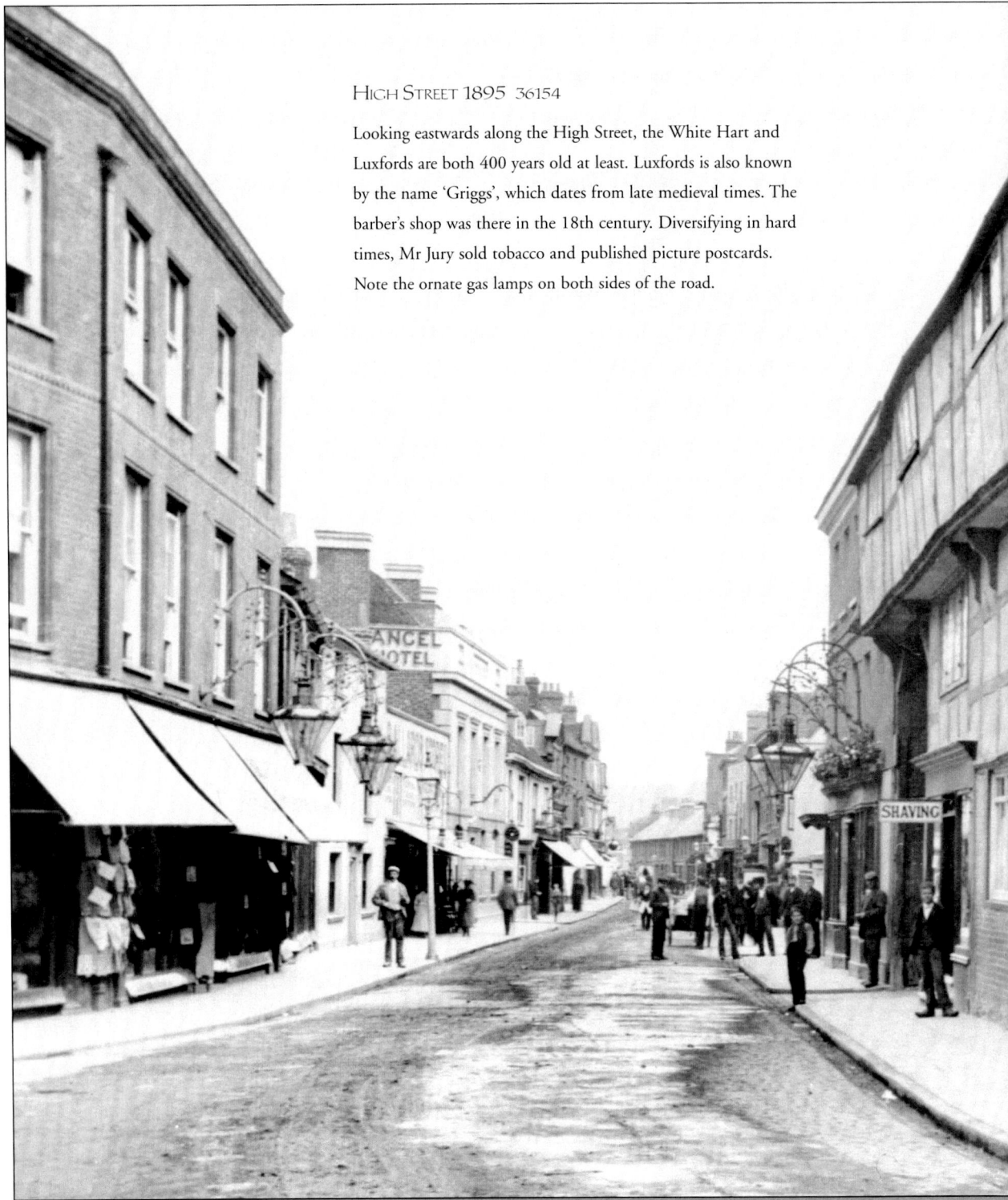

HIGH STREET 1895 36154

Looking eastwards along the High Street, the White Hart and Luxfords are both 400 years old at least. Luxfords is also known by the name 'Griggs', which dates from late medieval times. The barber's shop was there in the 18th century. Diversifying in hard times, Mr Jury sold tobacco and published picture postcards. Note the ornate gas lamps on both sides of the road.

THE HIGH STREET

THE HIGH STREET

ABOVE: HIGH STREET 1906 54163

The 'Upstairs, Downstairs' world of Edwardian Godalming. A pony and trap outside Burgess the grocer awaits its owner, while a shop boy stands guard. Burgess was the name above the window for over a century. Similarly durable, the London and County Bank on the left is still a bank (NatWest) and though Jones the ironmongers went in the 1960s (see trade advertisement on page 19), there had been an ironmonger's business there since the 18th century. The ivy clad wall left of centre was part of The Croft, home of Henry Marshall, four times mayor of Godalming; it gave its name to Croft Road, on the hillside behind the house.

RIGHT: HIGH STREET 1907 57513A

12 years after 36154, page 16, and little has altered. Luxford's has changed hands, and the gas lamps have gone. Note the Angel Hotel on the left, another of the main coaching inns.

The splendid 18th-century town house in the centre of photo 62238 (pages 14-15) was for most of the 19th century the home of the Stedman family, and for most of the 20th was the Post Office. It is now offices. The Red Lion, whose sign can just be seen in the same picture, is believed to have been the home of John Perrior, the town's first 'warden' when it received its borough charter in 1574. Henry Marshall, who was the town's first mayor of the reformed borough, in 1836, lived in The Croft, the ivy-covered building just left of centre in photo 54163, on the south side. His solicitors' office, directly opposite, still continues under his name.

A small town, Godalming has never had a large departmental store, but throughout the period of Frith's photos it came close with Burgess' Stores. Charles Burgess was a grocer whose business prospered to such an extent that, starting in 1873 with a single shop, by the 1900s he had shops in seven other local towns too. The main business by this time included a butcher's, a fishmonger's, a greengrocer's and a gift shop as

THE HIGH STREET

GEORGE JONES,
Furnishing, Builders' & General Ironmonger,
76, HIGH STREET, GODALMING.
GAS AND HOT WATER ENGINEER,
WHITESMITH, LOCKSMITH & BELLHANGER.

of those disappeared from the scene before the Second World War. They are a frequent sight in older photos, flat cap on head, basket on arm. It is ironic that some supermarkets are beginning to offer a delivery service again!

One change very noticeable in the street is that the early photos show it to have been paved with granite setts. 100 tons of these were bought in 1838 from Guildford, presumably surplus after the High Street there was so paved. Under an Act of 1825 Godalming had a board of Commissioners responsible for the paving, lighting and improvement of the streets. Despite the durability of the granite, there must have been some disadvantages because in 1913 they were all taken up and replaced by the then fashionable tarred wooden blocks. These too have their problems, for when wet they swell up and the pressure can cause whole sections to burst upwards. The street is now surfaced with tarmacadam, like almost everywhere else.

Inevitably there have been special occasions in the street. Two worth particular mention were in 1887 and 1897 - Queen Victoria's golden and diamond jubilees, when the street was closed and a party held in a marquee covering almost half its length, with an elaborate sham castle as entrance at the Pepperpot end. And this was then the main Portsmouth Road! Another was in 1892, when Queen Victoria's daughter in law, the Duchess of Albany, came to open the Meath Home (see photo G23014 on page 38-39) and was met at the Pepperpot, then the town hall, by the Mayor and other civic dignitaries. There were processions, often headed by the town band and the fire brigade in their uniforms, on the occasions of coronations, proclamation of royal accessions, and on fête days. On almost all such days the street would be decorated with flags, and crowds would gather to watch the procession pass by.

well as the grocery which can be seen in photo 54163. Burgess himself was six times Mayor, and his business survived until the 1960s. Other High Street stores also opened branches in neighbouring towns - Rea and Rothwell, both of them butchers; Gammons, drapers; and West, a photographer, are examples. Burgess was not of course the only grocer in the street. In Edwardian days, and indeed right up to about 1985, there were a number of grocers, greengrocers, dairies, butchers and bakers. With the arrival of the supermarkets most of these have foundered. Gone with them are the errand boys, though indeed most

The High Street

THE HIGH STREET

HIGH STREET c1965 G23085
59 years later than view 54163, page 18, and the bank looks very much the same. The little shop to the left of it, then Mullards Southern Rentals, is interesting - at one time it was the entrance to a wool merchants' premises, and until fairly recently there was a small crane above for lifting bales of wool into the first floor store. Fine Fare, extreme left, was Godalming's first supermarket.

The High Street

High Street 1906 54163A

A little nearer to the middle of the High Street, and there are more fancy gas lamps to be seen. The building on the left, called Manchester House, has been a draper's for over a century - successively Enticknap, Wyeth and Everett, Darking's, McIlroys, Aspens, and now Mackays (see advertisement page 24). The building opposite bears the date 1663, though the very decorative windows may be a little more recent. At one time there was similar glazing on the ground floor.

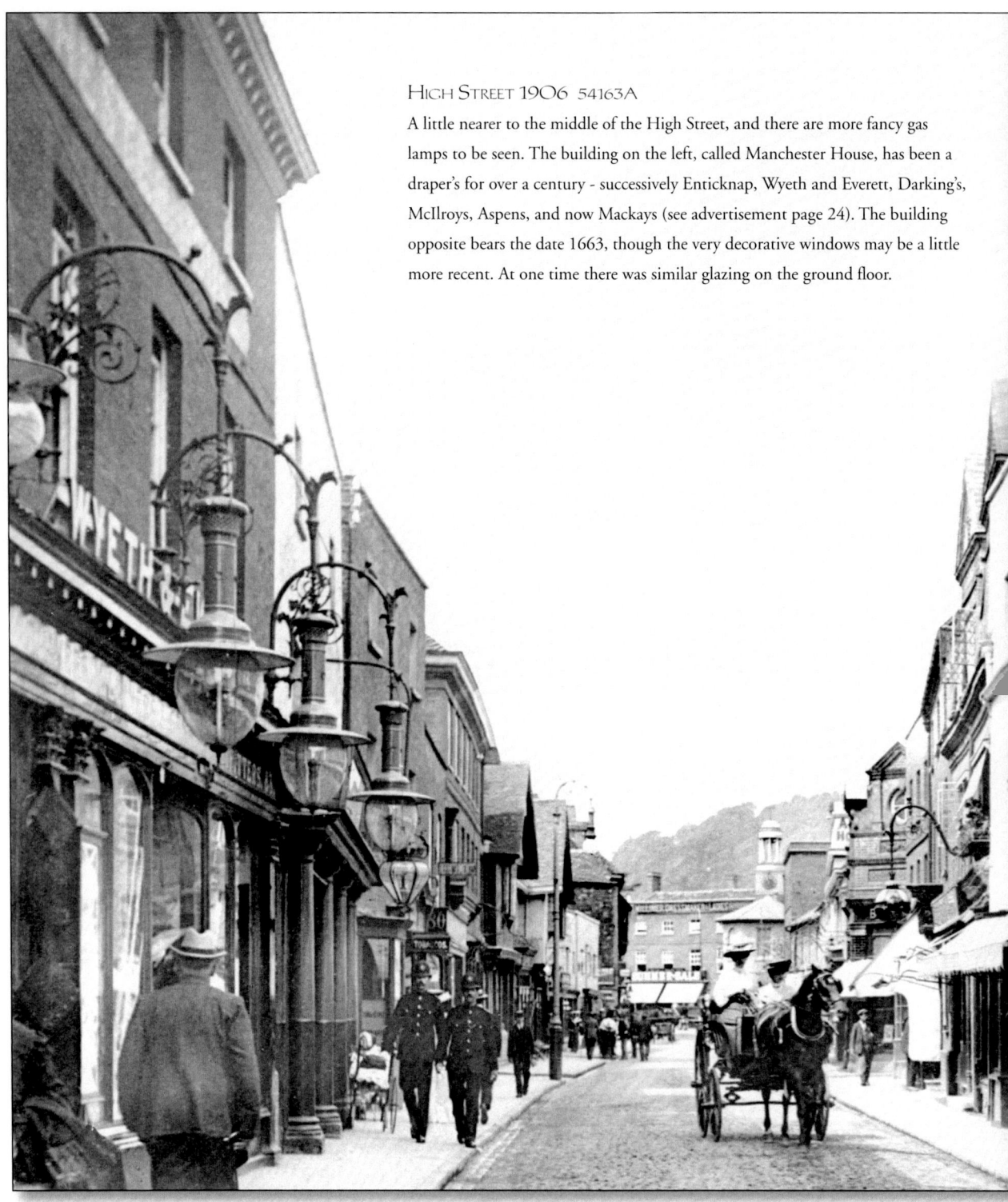

The High Street

The High Street

Right: High Street 1933 85497

Woolworths on the left - proudly boasting that nothing in the store cost over 6d - and W H Smith on the right, are still on the same sites nearly 70 years after this photo was taken. And Edwards pharmacy, extreme right, became Boots the Chemists, who moved later to the corner of Moss Lane. Note the single-side parking in operation.

BUY YOUR **Spring and Summer Outfit** AT **DARKING BROS.**

BEST STYLE. VALUE. SERVICE in the District.

For LADIES' COSTUMES and MILLINERY.

Men's and Boys' "Ready-to-wear" SUITS.

RAINCOATS.

HATS.

HOSIERY.

Our "Famous" All-Wool Gabardine COSTUME. Three shades. From **42/11**

Manchester House Godalming

Phone **145**

EXPERT TAILORING ON THE PREMISES

Smart "All-Wool" TWEED SUIT. Well Tailored. Half Sizes. From **42/-**

GODALMING
The High Street

LEFT: DETAIL FROM 54163A (PAGES 22-23)

The High Street

High Street c1965 G23109

Looking west again, the large building left of centre was the third of the great coaching inns, the Great George (to distinguish it from its smaller neighbour). The bottle and jug department on the corner continued to sell alcohol until recently, as a wine shop. The remaining buildings on the right are the most altered part of the street, having been demolished and rebuilt twice since 1900.

The High Street

The High Street

The High Street

High Street c1955 G23032

Looking now to the east: Timothy Whites and Taylors, now Martins newsagents and the Post Office, span two buildings. The larger of the two buildings was at one time a pub called The George. The smaller, on the left, was the scene of a double murder in 1817, when one night George Chennel and William Chalcraft, after drinking, returned to Chennell's father's home and bludgeoned the old man and his housekeeper to death, seeking more money for drink. They were publicly hung on the Lammas Land.

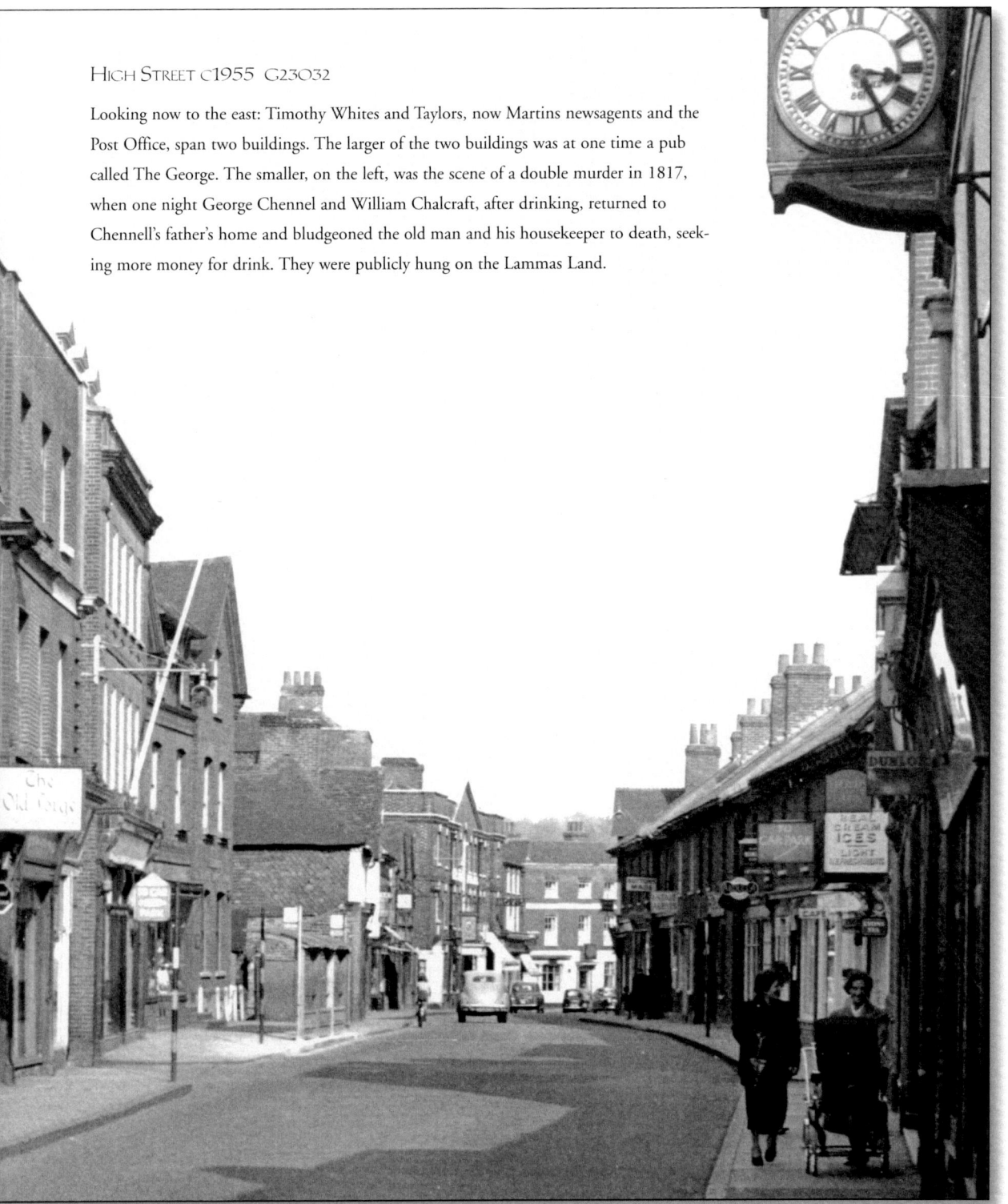

The High Street

The High Street

High Street c1955 G23047

This photo of the street, looking west, shows clearly its 'slightly sinuous' line. On the left is the beginning of Queen Street, and the advertisement on the wall above it was for the Victoria Motor works, in the Victoria Hall, latterly used as auction rooms. Note the painted sign of the Woolpack pub on the right - it was so called for centuries but at the end of the 20th century was renamed 'Sports 2000', and has now, 5 years later, been renamed again - as Number 28.

Byways and Buildings

ABOVE: THE CAR PARK 1956 G23076

In 1956 Crown Court, a medieval weavers' court, which had survived intact for centuries, was broken through to make an exit from the new car park. Only a score or so years later, this exit was closed as it led straight into the High Street, and caused traffic difficulties. Though the arch was attractively built, and seemed like a good idea at the time, there is no recalling the piece of history destroyed for such a short-lived benefit.

RIGHT: HOLLOWAY HILL 1910 62245

If the High Street is Godalming's spine, a number of other streets form the limbs, but only three of those which join the High Street are of equal antiquity with it: Ockford Road, and Church Street, near the western end, and Bridge Street, which forms a continuation of High Street, at its eastern end.

Rather less ancient, the name of Wharf Street implies a connection with the navigation, which arrived in 1764. The others were mostly developments of formerly private entrances. Moss Lane, Great George Street, and Queen Street date from the 19th century, and Angel Court and Pound Close from the 20th, though the latter grew on the little Pound Lane which formerly led to the town forge. Crown Court is a rather special mixture of ancient and modern. Taking its name from a pub, the Crown, which once occupied buildings on the high street frontage, this former medieval weavers' court had only a narrow pedestrian access, until in 1956 it was opened up by demolition of the north and south sides. The purpose was to form a vehicle exit from the then new car park. Two ancient streets which formerly joined the High Street, Mill Lane and Holloway Hill, both at the western end, were separated from it when the inner relief road, Flambard Way, was built in the 1990s.

Byways and Buildings

It is apt that photo 62245 includes a group of schoolgirls - for in that year, 1910, the predecessor of St Hilary's school was set up in a house just out of sight to the left. St Hilary's is now located a hundred yards or so further north. Gertrude Jekyll records in 'Old West Surrey' that in the late 18th century smuggled brandy would be brought from the west country, taken down Holloway Hill by night, and sold in the town. Until the late 19th century there was only a farmhouse on the hill. By 1911 there were 101 houses, and now there are many times that number.

ORDNANCE SURVEY MAP

ORDNANCE SURVEY MAP

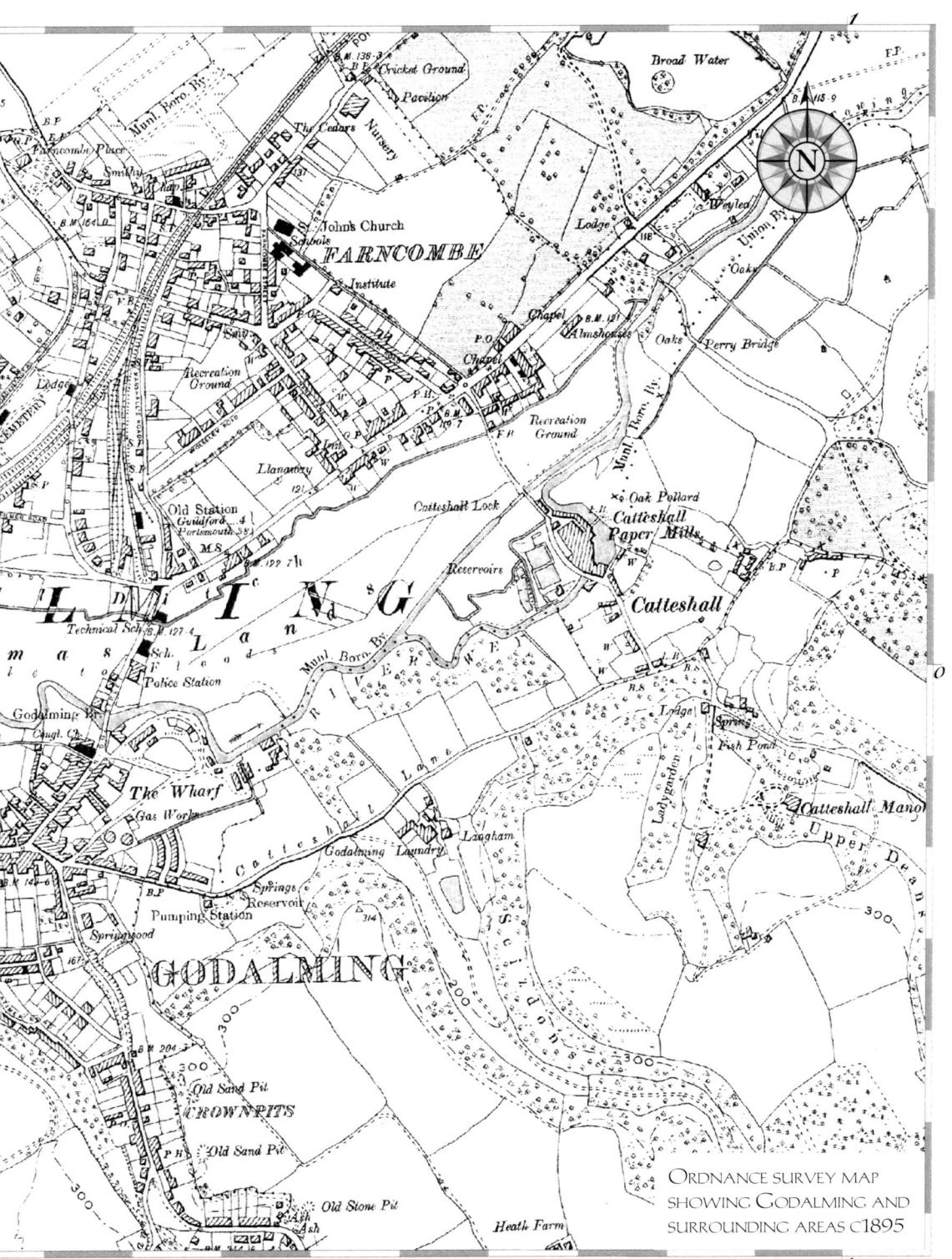

Ordnance survey map showing Godalming and surrounding areas c1895

Byways and Buildings

ABOVE: CHURCH STREET 1906 57049

In Edwardian days cyclists frequented Godalming, especially at weekends. There was a demand for teashops, and Church Street had three - one is on the left here. Also very popular was the sending of picture postcards, which served people much as the telephone does today - Eatons paper shop, on the left, claimed to have the largest selection.

RIGHT: CHURCH STREET 1906 57050

Three of Church Street's five pubs are in this photo - the Corn Meter extreme left, the Star centre left, and the Live and Let Live just beyond the archway on the right. The arch led to the rear of the Angel Hotel yard, owned at that time by John Jasper Taylor, who also had a temperance hotel, Deanery House, further down Church Street.

RIGHT:
CHURCH STREET c1955 G23036

Byways and Buildings

Church Street links the parish church and the Pepperpot. Part of the church is Saxon, and it is believed that the wider area of the High Street in which the Pepperpot stands was the focus of local government for a lot longer than there has been a building on the site. It seems reasonable to conclude that the street, as a route, is at least 1000 years old. The buildings are probably only half that age. The date 1086 is over the door of Church House, the white building at the far end of the street, in photos 57049 and 57050, but that probably refers to the date of the Domesday survey, when the area was held by Ranulf Flambard. He was financial adviser to King William Rufus and was later Dean of Salisbury. On his death his lands in the area passed to the Dean and Chapter of Salisbury, and were thereafter known as the deanery manor. Apart from the names over the shops, and the loss of the tree outside Church House, most of Church street has looked very much the same since Victorian times or earlier. At one time there were five pubs and at least three teashops in this short street; now only one of each remains, The Star, whose white upstairs windows can be seen on the left side in photo 57050, and a small sandwich bar opposite.

At the end of Church Street furthest from the Pepperpot, it is joined by Borough Road, Station Road and Westbrook Road. The West Brook is the little River Ock, but the name early became associated with the mill which stands at the confluence of the Ock and the Wey - possibly one of the three mills in Godalming mentioned in the Domesday survey - and also with the house and 'small manor' just to the west. The small manor earns its place in history for it was for a time the home of the Oglethorpe family, of whom the most famous was General James Oglethorpe, acknowledged as the founding father of the colony of Georgia in the USA. The house was later owned by a quack doctor, Nathaniel Godbold, then by Lord Brassey, whose main interest lay in the fact that it lay on the route of his new railway to provide a direct route to Portsmouth, and finally in 1892 by the Countess of Meath. She bought it to provide a home for women and girls suffering from epilepsy. Photographed for Friths in 1955 (photo G23014, page 38), it has been modernised and continues to provide for epileptics as she wished.

Photograph G23036 shows clearly the antiquity of the former cottages, now all shops, lining narrow Church Street. In a small way, it also shows the continuity of some businesses. The teashop, Dicky Thorn's, on the right in photo 57050 in 1906, was established in 1897 - but was still there in 1955 (the shop with a pedestrian outside). It continued until 1973. The Star pub too is in both photos, and that continues to this day.

The classical exterior of Meath Home (see G23014) masks its 17th century origins. It was then known as Westbrook, and a century later it was the home for some years of General James Oglethorpe, who founded the colony of Georgia in the USA. In 1734 he brought to England ten Yamacraw Indians, who stayed here with him. His sisters were Jacobite sympathisers, and while he was in America they had the house fortified - the townsfolk were likely to be hostile in the event of conflict. In 1892 the house became a home for epileptic girls and women.

Byways and Buildings

As with Crown Court in the 20th century, Queen Street could be created in the 19th only after the demolition of shops on the High Street frontage. This happened in 1897, the year of the diamond jubilee, and it was apparently at first intended that it should be called Jubilee Street. Once the street was opened, development was fairly rapid, and by the time photo 62242, page 40, was taken in 1910 it was complete. It included the Baptist church, the fire station, a photographer's studio and the large Victoria Hall, as well as many semi-detached houses. The hall was used by a motor works, and in 1907 the 'Victoria' motor car was assembled there, a 10/12 horsepower tourer.

'Crownpits' is a corruption of an Old English word, crumb, meaning bent or crooked, via 'crompett' (1548). On the right in view 36163, page 44, are two pubs next door to each other; both went in the 60s. The Queen's Head is now a private house, while the Three Crowns was demolished and four town houses (which all have 'crown' in their names) built on the site.

Like Church Street, Bridge Street at the other end of town had its pubs: there were six, and four breweries. Also like Church Street, only one pub remains, and the large tree that once formed such an attractive 'closer' to the view was felled in the 60s. But unlike Church Street, there have been more buildings demolished and replaced here than anywhere else in town. About a third of the buildings on the right in photo G23029, page 49, went in the 1980s, and most of those on the left in photo G23046, page 49, were built between 1850 and 1908. An obvious exception is the timber-framed building in the middle, probably Tudor, the last remaining part of a large complex variously called The Greate House, King John's Hunting Lodge, and Bridgers, burned down in 1869. Bridge Street was formerly Water Lane - a stream used to run down it to the river. Though driven underground, the stream is still very much there, as the builders of the new superstore found in the 1990s, when their digging broke into it and much flooding of the site followed.

In Frith's day, the two largest - or at any rate tallest - buildings in Bridge Street were the Sun Brewery and the Municipal Buildings. The four-storey former Sun Steam Brewery, built in 1865, and seen on the right in photo G23046, page 47, still dominates the street. The Municipal Buildings, in photo 59949, were an aggregation of three elements: Stone House, the imposing former home of Thomas White, a brewer who became mayor in 1869; the bargate stone public hall, built as a private venture in 1861; and the new offices built in 1908. These were designed by J H Norris, the borough surveyor. The three elements have now been joined by a fourth, for behind the buildings in the photo are the much larger Waverley Borough Council offices, built in the 1980s.

Byways and Buildings

Meath Home c1955 G23014

Byways and Buildings

Byways and Buildings

QUEEN STREET 1910 62242

The width of Queen Street shows that it was of fairly recent construction. But its appearance is wholly different today, having been cut in two by the inner relief road, Flambard Way. Note the car outside the Victoria Hall, at that time a motor works. Could this be the Victoria tourer, which was built there?

Byways and Buildings

Constitutional Club 1895 36152

This building had very elegant mock-Elizabethan red brick chimneys, demolished in the 1960s. At the same time the large porch, with balcony above, was also demolished, supposedly for road widening. The tea dealers', just to the right of the carts, became the local British Legion's headquarters in 1920, but they recently relinquished it and in 1994 it opened as Godalming's first 20th century pub, the Old Wharf.

GODALMING Byways and Buildings

Byways and Buildings

ABOVE: CROWN PITS 1895 36163

RIGHT: TOWN END STREET 1906 54692

Before this street was built, following the line of an old footpath, 'Town End' was a large field used for fêtes, and sometimes a circus. The houses were built in brick; half a century earlier, before the railway, they would have been built of bargate stone. Today, the houses have hardly changed, but the street is almost permanently lined with parked cars - there is no space for garages.

Byways and buildings

Byways and Buildings

Byways and Buildings

Municipal Buildings 1908 59949

The Borough Hall has been described as dull, but given the task facing the designer, who had to merge a private house, a public hall, and some new offices, the result is really very successful. The triple arches of the entrance, the sash windows of the first floor, and the gable above, match corresponding features of the old hall, blending the two frontages into a satisfying whole. Since 1908 the double door entrance of the hall has been turned into a window, cleverly imitating the three windows to its left. In the 1900s the hall was used for the first cinema in the town.

Byways and Buildings

ABOVE: TRADE ADVERTISEMENT FOR THE SUN BREWERY

RIGHT: BRIDGE STREET C1955 G23046

Until nearly the end of the 20th century there was still two-way traffic in this most changed of all Godalming's streets. Unchanged, however, are the four-storey former Sun Steam Brewery on the right, and the building with the oriel window on the left. Built as the Godalming Liberal Club in 1878, its terracotta façade must have been startling when new.

Byways and Buildings

Left: Bridge Street c1965 G23029

A view of the southeast side of Bridge Street. While many of the buildings on the right remain, several were pulled down in the 1980s and their sites now form part of a supermarket car park. On the credit side, however, the car park wall incorporates excellent modern wrought iron sculptures, and lying as it does opposite the municipal offices, the car park looks like a town square.

GODALMING
River, Road and Rail

River, Road and Rail

Catteshall Lock 1908 59954

The Wey and Godalming navigations were 'barge' canals - built before the narrow boat's 70 feet by 6 feet 10 inches became the standard. This photo shows its width clearly. Since the Wey and Arun Canal closed in 1861 this lock has been the most southerly of the connected canal system of Britain, and the last before reaching Godalming Wharf. The town can be seen in the distance across the Lammas Land. Commercial traffic on this part of the Wey ceased in 1925, but as the photo shows, well before then pleasure boating had begun to take its place.

River, Road and Rail

ABOVE: RIVER WEY CAMPING GROUND 1908 59956

One suspects that Frith's photos of the river shown on these pages may have been commissioned by Mr Leroy to sell to his customers - he appears in this one too, in a Canadian canoe, fashionable at the time. The camping ground was just to the east of the boathouse. Though camping was already enjoyed, Baden-Powell's book 'Scouting for boys' was published in the same year, and may have increased its popularity.

Until well into the 18th century English roads were dreadful - unsurfaced, rutted, muddy and indirect. Carriage of heavy loads, such as timber, was difficult and expensive. Oak from the Sussex forests destined for building in London had to be transported on roads through the wealden clay which were 'all but impassable for much of the year'. Transport by water was much easier. In 1654 - well before the canal building boom - the River Wey was made navigable to Guildford. A century later the Wey navigation was extended to Godalming. It proved profitable, and despite the coming of the railway continued to carry goods until well into the 20th century. Its principal use today is for pleasure craft and fishing.

The Victorians were very fond of pleasure boating, and in June 1895, the 'Surrey Advertiser' reported that some gentlemen had combined to purchase boats for hire and that six boats had been brought from Reading. Shortly after, Mr A Leroy established a boatshed by the Catteshall Road bridge (see 59953). About 1910 he built a house between the shed and the bridge. He is the man seen here rowing the skiff. His business must have been popular - as witness the number of skiffs and punts in the photo - and the Farncombe Boathouse is still with us. Sometimes his customers would fall into the river or the lock, and have to be rescued. His wife was not pleased at having to deal with wet clothes so often!

Canal travel was never very swift. When in the second half of the 18th century properly constructed and surfaced roads appeared - the turnpikes - the journey time from London to Portsmouth, the country's main naval base, was reduced to two days. Godalming lay almost

River, Road and Rail

LEROY'S BOATHOUSE 1908 59953

exactly half way. No traveller would willingly risk the dangers of continuing through the night, especially when only a few miles to the south lay the heights of the Devil's Punch Bowl, difficult enough for the horses at the best of times, and the possibility of a hold up by highwaymen. The town's inns therefore became regular staging posts. The main four, from east to west, were the King's Arms, the Great George, the Angel, and the White Hart, but there were many smaller inns where a traveller could put up for the night.

The King's Arms is the building just to the left of the cyclists in photograph G23033, page 54. The last remaining of Godalming's coaching inns still trading, it was the most prestigious of them, and is a good deal older than its 1753 brick façade suggests. The arms on the inn sign are those of Henry VIII. A royal visitor in 1698 was Peter the Great, Czar of all the Russias, who had been to Portsmouth to study the navy. His entourage, whom the diarist John Evelyn's butler later described as 'right nasty', apparently consumed a great deal of food and drink. Later, 'Accommodation', the London coach, ran regularly between here and the White Horse in Piccadilly; the fare was half a guinea.

River, Road and Rail

High Street c1955 G23033

The large building on the right of view 36153 (pages 56-57) was the Great George Inn. It was originally the George and Dragon, abbreviated to the George, but when it closed for a period the building next but one, nearer the centre, opened as a pub also under the name of the George. Confusion was avoided by their customers calling the larger inn, the Great George, and the other the Little George! Both closed a long time ago, but the shop on the extreme right, the bottle and jug department of the Great George, continued as an off-licence. Opposite, the butcher's shop has the open display typical of the period. No wonder diseases spread so readily then.

The coaching era was great while it lasted, but the railway reached Godalming in 1849. When the engineering difficulty of crossing the marshy Wey valley was overcome in 1859, and the railway extended to Portsmouth, the day of the stagecoach was ended. Godalming, by-passed, went to sleep for a while.

Godalming's first railway station, 1845, was on the Farncombe side of the river. When the line was extended to the coast, a new station was built near Hatch House, Mill Lane (see 54682, pages 60-61). For many years both stations continued to be used, known appropriately as 'Godalming Old', and 'Godalming New'. Until the 1960s, the 'New' station continued to be lit by gas, the result of a 100 years' contract with the gas company. The attractive cast iron lamp standards, twisted like barley sugar, were scrapped and replaced, alas, by plain steel standards, already tatty. The station itself, however, was well renovated a few years ago, thanks to a local firm of brewers with offices nearby.

River, Road and Rail

Boating on the River Wey 1908 59957

Here Mr Leroy has left the ladies to it. Perhaps the idea was to show that boating was not to be thought a solely male activity! Punting seems less common nowadays, except perhaps at Cambridge, though punts can still be hired at Farncombe.

River, Road and Rail

High Street 1895 36153

River, Road and Rail

River, Road, and Rail

River, Road and Rail

The White Hart
1906 54683

The White Hart was a fine old coaching inn dating back at least to 1570. The large arch on the left is where coaches would draw into the yard behind. In 1906 it was used by a builder. It is said that in their day both Drake and Nelson stopped here - possible, but undocumented and impossible to prove. What is documented, is that in 1734 General Oglethorpe brought here to dine the ten Yamacraw Red Indians he had staying with him at Westbrook. The effect was comparable to having men from Mars to tea today - word quickly spread and a crowd of the curious soon gathered.

River, Road and Rail

River, Road and Rail

The Railway Station 1906
54682

BRABNER MAP GODALMING

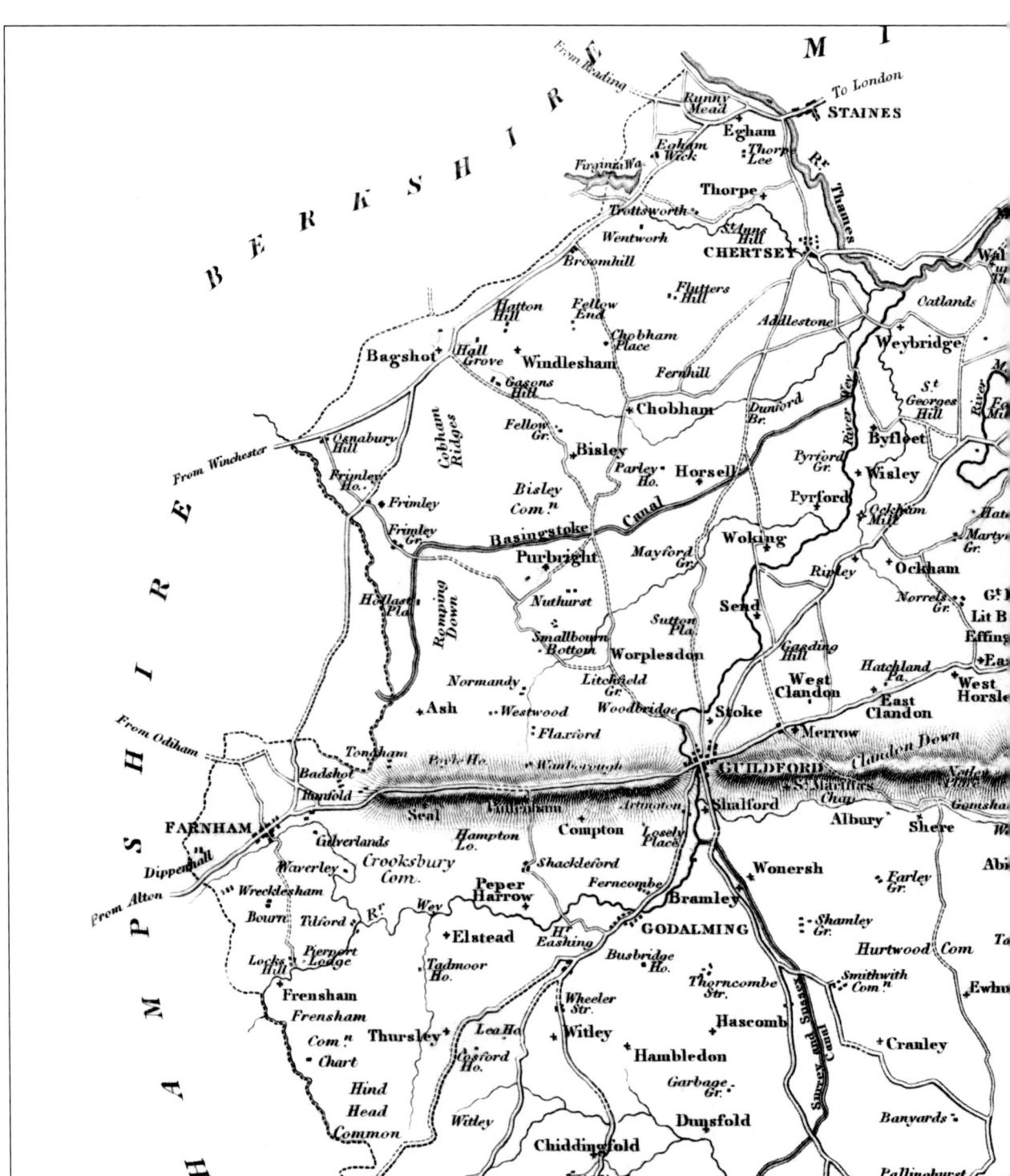

BRABNER MAP

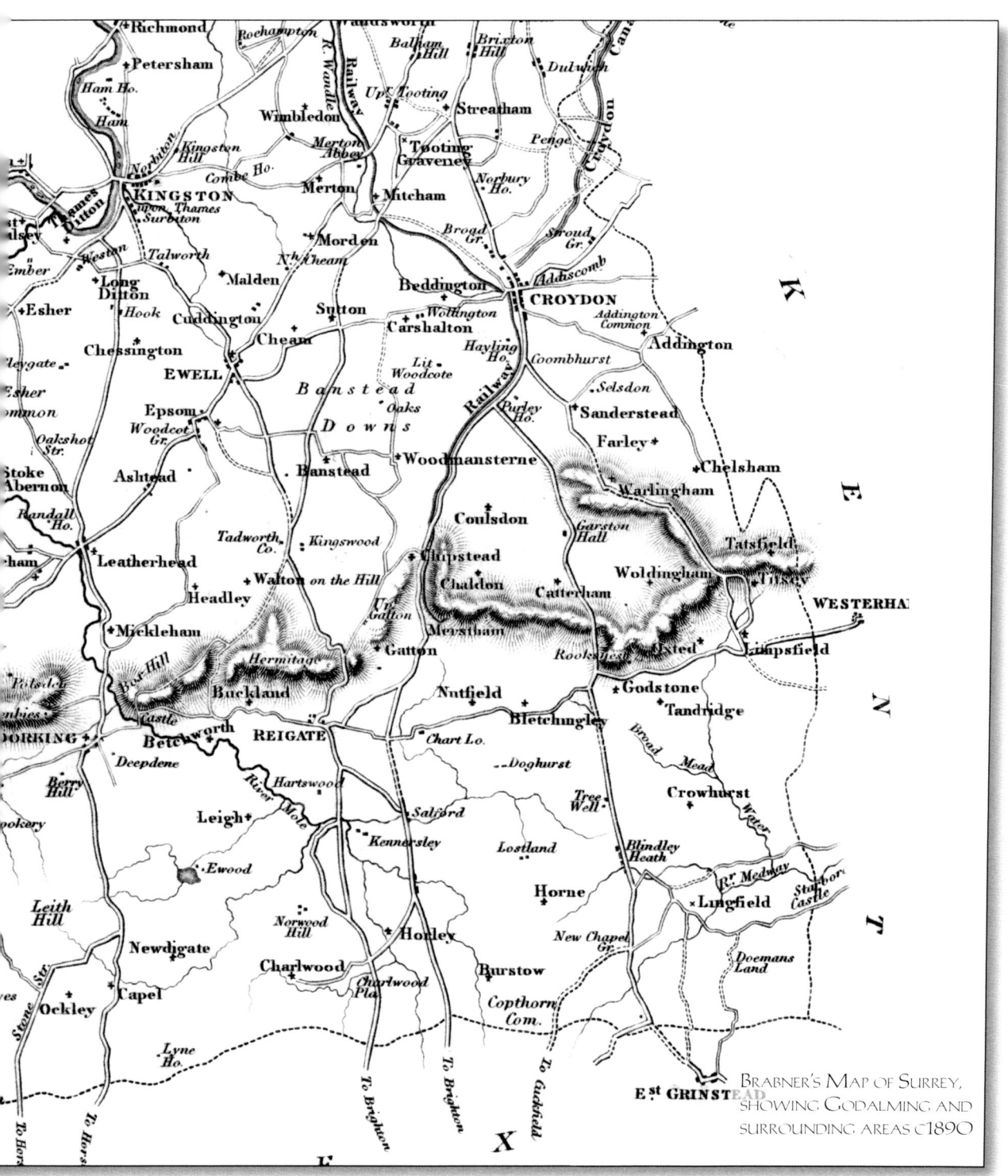

Brabner's Map of Surrey, showing Godalming and surrounding areas c1890

Industry

The Town from New Way 1907 57510

This photograph shows the parish church spire rivalled by the chimney of Rea and Fisher's oak bark leather tannery, noted for its smell. The smaller chimney is that of Allen, Solly and Company's steam hosiery factory, the building on the left.

Nowadays, Godalming's appearance is much like many other town's on the outer periphery of the greater London area - a commuter's suburb, based on an old market town. But this appearance belies its history - for centuries, it was an industrial town, quite as much so as the wool and cotton towns of Yorkshire and Lancashire. Indeed, wool was the town's main source of income throughout the medieval period. In the early 17th century fashions changed and demand fell away for its standard product, blue 'kersey' - a kind of coarse narrow cloth, woven from long wool, and usually ribbed. For a while there was a good deal of unemployment, but the townsfolk turned to the recently invented stocking knitting frame and a considerable cottage industry grew up. There are still cottages in the town where the upper floors had extra large windows, the better to enable the stocking knitters to work at their frames for as long as daylight lasted. Several families might have worked together, with the menfolk working the heavy frames, the children winding the yarn, and the women seaming and finishing the stockings. In time the industry became more organised, and was carried out in purpose-built factories. Then even

Industry

The Old Forge, Pound Lane 1910 62243

During the coaching era the need to re-shoe horses must have made the blacksmith essential. The forge in Godalming was situated very centrally, in Pound Lane, where Record Corner is now. In the 1860s the smith added to his business by opening a beerhouse, appropriately named the Three Horseshoes, next to the forge. Also nearby was a whitesmith, Mr H Lewer who was also a gasfitter and electrician.

Left: Pullman's Mill 1910 62248

Industry

this industry drifted away to other towns further north, notably Nottingham, and the last link with the wool trade ended when the firm of Alan Paine closed its factory in the dying years of the 20th century.

While wool was pre-eminent, other industries occupied the people. Perhaps originally because of the ready availability locally of oak bark (which is rich in tannin, and produces the best quality leather, though slowly) the curing of leather kept many in work. Pullman's Westbrook Mill produced soft, chamois type leathers; Gay & Co in Ockford Road worked on small skins such as rabbit; and Rea and Fisher's by the railway, the heavier hides. It was said that a blind man arriving by train would know he was in Godalming by the stink!

At the end of the 19th century the town was at its most industrial stage. With its leather mills, woollen factories, breweries and quarries, and with a paper mill at Catteshall, it was not a pleasant place. In 1890, a newly appointed County Council public health inspector reported on 'the rush of offensive liquid and solid matter from Rea's tannery', and 'liquid filth of Godalming's slaughterhouses' polluting the river. By 1895 however, he could report that Godalming was one of 24 places with sewage treatment works recently completed or in course of completion.

Formerly known as Westbrook and Salgasson Mills, there has been a mill on the site of Pullman's for perhaps a thousand years (see 62248, page 65). Leather working probably began here in the 18th century, and was continued by the Pullman firm from 1878 until 1952. In the early years of motoring the company, diversifying, introduced 'Pullman's Non Skid Bands', for wrapping motor tyres in wet weather. But their most interesting innovation was the use of electricity in 1881, to light the mill and to power street lighting and even house lighting in Godalming itself. The spur was high charges by the gas company. John Pullman was a borough councillor, and it seems to have been on his initiative that the council tried the new power. Thus Godalming became the first place in the world to have a public electricity supply. It did not last - there were too few customers, the equipment gave trouble, and the gas company reduced its prices, so the town reverted to gas.

INDUSTRY

MILL LANE 1910 62239

When this photo was taken there were frequent horse wagons calling at Hatch Mill, just out of the photo to the right. They brought grain and took away flour, all in heavy sacks which had to be manhandled. Note the slope into the river; this enabled horses to be led to the water to drink, and carts to be taken right into the water in dry weather, to swell up the wooden wheels and thus keep them tight within their iron rims.

Industry

Then there was quarrying. The local bargate sandstone is durable and many of the town's buildings made full use of it. There were several quarries in the vicinity and the work went on until the Second World War, though it had been in decline as a building material ever since the railway brought cheaper bricks from the Midlands. Fortunately perhaps, the stone proved too soft for road making, or by now the local hills would have been heavily scarred if not levelled!

There was brewing of beer. There were at least seven breweries in the town, four of them in Bridge Street alone. Hops grew well locally, and there were plenty of pubs to be supplied - 22 from the Anchor in Ockford Road to the Half Moon in Meadrow, six more in Church Street, two in Mill Lane, one at the forge in Pound Lane, two at Crownpits, and others in Farncombe.

And of course there were the usual trades to be found in any such town. There was blacksmithing at the forge in Pound Lane, with a whitesmith (who finished metalware rather than forging it) almost next door, and another where the hardware store of Robert Dyas is currently. The last saddler who made his wares on the premises, at the foot of Holloway Hill, closed his business at the end of the 1950s. Of the three mills for grinding corn mentioned in the Domesday survey, Catteshall Mill was converted to the making of paper for a while. With the passage of time much of the evidence of the industrial past has faded. It is as well that we have photographs to record the old days.

Industry

The Flour Mill 1908 59952

Hatch Mill is in the oldest part of the town, may well be the oldest mill site and was the last mill to operate in Godalming. It closed in the 1960s. The building has now been converted to offices, and the mill pool filled in and turned into a car park.

The Churches

The Saxons' foundation of Godalming was not far removed in time from the landing of St Augustine in Kent, (which led to their conversion to Christianity) and it was not long before there was a church nearby, at Tuesley just south of the town.

It had initially been a shrine to the great god Tiw, but was continued under the new regime. Eventually it fell into disuse, and crumbled. The foundations were excavated in the late 1860s, revealing a chancel and nave, whose outlines may still be seen. Perhaps it was too inconveniently situated up on the hill, away from the town, for it was not long before the townsfolk built a new church, the forerunner of the present parish church of St Peter and St Paul. Some of that early building was incorporated into the church as we know it today. There is work of every century from the 9th to the 20th in it, though the 21st century is yet too young to have made its contribution. The list of rectors and vicars begins with Ulmaer, in the time of King Edward the Confessor. The oak parish chest has been dated at 1200. The tall graceful spire was built in the 14th century; its proportions remind one of Salisbury Cathedral's, though it is much smaller of course. The comparison is perhaps not too fanciful - Godalming's rectory manor was at that time held by the Dean and Chapter of Salisbury. Fragments of medieval wall paintings have been found, including one of St John the Baptist. The ceiling bosses in the nave are painted with coats of arms of the Tudor period. More recently, the building was twice 'restored' in the 19th century.

In the 19th century, too, the great tithes of Godalming were used by the Church Commissioners to endow three new rectories of Farncombe, Busbridge and Shackleford, and in 1934 a 'daughter' church, St Mark's, was built on Ockford Ridge.

The established church did not however have things all its own way. Godalming has a long history of non-conformity, and the Unitarians, Society of Friends ('Quakers'), Baptists, Congregationalists, Wesleyan Methodists and The Salvation Army all have, or had, their own churches. The building in Mint Street currently (2005) used by the Salvation Army was used by the Congregationalists until in 1867 they decided they needed a bigger church: by October 1868 the money had been raised, the church designed, built and opened on a site by the Town Bridge! The house next door was bought for a manse; it was demolished in the 1960s, and the site used for the new public library. The Congregationalists were followed in the Mint Street building by the Wesleyan Methodists, until they in turn built their own new church in Bridge Road in 1903. For three-quarters of a century they worshipped in their separate ways on opposite sides of the Town Bridge, until in 1977 they came together as the Godalming United Church, and sold the older building.

The Congregational church was in use for 109 years, the last service being held on Christmas morning 1977. The railings were taken to help the war effort in 1940, and the spire was removed as unsafe in the 1970s. After closure as a church, the building was used for auctions for some years, but has recently been refurbished and used for a restaurant.

THE CHURCHES

THE PARISH CHURCH 1922 71782

The parish church was first established by the Saxons on a sandy knoll well above flood level. This photo shows it from the north, across the river from the Phillips Memorial Recreation Ground, opened in April 1914. The tombstones in the churchyard have been left standing, against the modern trend, leaving the church in its traditional setting.

The Churches

LEFT: THE CONGREGATIONAL CHURCH 1898 41791

RIGHT: BUSBRIDGE CHURCH 1906 53573
The churchyard at Busbridge is full of memorials, including one to Gertrude Jekyll, the great gardener, who lived nearby at Munstead. But the church is itself a memorial, paid for by Emma Ramsden of Busbridge Hall to commemorate her first husband. Designed by Sir George Gilbert Scott RA, it was built in 1866 in bargate stone lined with chalk.

THE ROMAN CATHOLIC CHURCH 1907 57269
There is a fable that this church was built high on the hillside so that even its small spire would be higher and thus nearer to God than the Anglican church in the valley! It is however fact that its 28 steps are a deterrent to the elderly and infirm, and there is no space for car parking. In 1967 a new church was opened in Milford.

The Churches

The Wesleyan Church and School 1903 49196

Like the Congregationalists before them, the Methodists set up their new church by the river (see 49196). They felt a need to fill 'The Surrey wilderness', an area of under-representation for Methodism, and significant funding came from a fund set up by Hugh Price Hughes: unfortunately, he died before it was finished, and the church was named after him as a memorial. The gardens were laid out to a design by Gertrude Jekyll.

The Roman Catholic Church, discounting the 1000 years or so before King Henry VIII separated the Anglican church from it, has a relatively short history in Godalming. From 1899 mass was celebrated in a corrugated iron building in Croft Road, but in 1904 the Godalming Catholic Parish was created and a new priest, Father Hyland, was appointed. His lodgings at 36 Croft Road were opposite an empty hillside and he decided to build a new permanent church there. This was completed in 1906. He was probably its principal benefactor, and when he died in 1950 was buried under the Sanctuary.

Godalming Schools

The origins of schooling in Godalming are obscure. No doubt there were 'Dame' schools from perhaps as early as the 17th century, but the first documentary evidence is a reference to a school for 50 poor boys, contained in a letter written in 1715 to the Society For The Promotion Of Christian Knowledge (SPCK). Apart from dame schools, education was pretty well left to the Church - or rather churches, for the various non-conformist persuasions were as active in provision of schools as the established church.

What begins as teaching of religion soon becomes the teaching of a much wider curriculum. A great, and at times bitter, rivalry developed in Godalming, mainly between the established church's National, or 'Bell' school (after the system devised for mass education by a Dr Bell), and the non-conformist Lancastrian or 'British' school. In about 1813 the former moved into purpose-built schoolrooms in The Mint: there were also two cottages, one for the schoolmaster and one to be let to subsidise his pay. The cottages still exist, with the covered passageway which led into the school yard. Under Dr Bell's system, the master taught a number of older children, called monitors, who then taught smaller groups of younger children what they had just learned themselves. Thus many children could be taught at minimal cost.

It seems however that the Mint schoolrooms were badly built, because by 1840 there were large cracks in the walls and when on Sundays some 220 children were accommodated, there were real fears of collapse! At about this time, however, two other events occurred which led to a big improvement. The first was that the Borough joined with the Borough of Guildford for Poor Law purposes. The new Union built a new, large workhouse in Guildford (its infirmary later became St Luke's Hospital), and this made the Godalming workhouse in Moss Lane redundant. The second event was the restoration of the Parish Church; during the very extensive disruption caused by the building works, the vicar, seeking a temporary alternative place for church services, rented the empty workhouse, less than 100 yards away. Although already half a century old, it was very soundly built, with wide, high rooms, big windows, and cellars below. The vicar, the Rev J Bull, saw its potential for a school and somewhat impetuously signed the contract to buy it before he had the money to pay for it. Coming on top of 'soaring costs of the Parish Church renovations' this put him in severe financial straits. The money was however eventually found, and the workhouse served well for a school for the next 69 years. At the time it was hoped that it would provide accommodation for 528 children, and that this would 'counteract the unfair and proselytising efforts of the enemies of the church' - the British School operating in Bridge Road. In 1910 the old workhouse was finally demolished and the Moss Lane School we know today was built, to a very good standard of construction and equipment.

Godalming Schools

The British Schools 1905 53241

A meeting in the King's Arms in 1812 concerned with 'promoting the education of the labouring classes' led to the building of this school in 1813. It followed the non-conformists' 'Lancastrian' system, and was financed mainly by subscriptions and a penny a week from each child. The founders included the Warden, Thomas Haines, and local businessmen.

The British School in Bridge Road was not the only non-conformist school: in 1879 the Congregationalists added a new schoolhouse at the rear of their church, and the Methodists had a school hall, to hold 300 scholars, attached to their new church in 1903 (this is clearly shown in photo 49196, on page 73).

Other schools were established in the Borough: St John's Street, Farncombe in 1856; Busbridge in 1868; then George Road, Farncombe; and Meadrow in 1906. And there were private, fee-paying schools - the Grammar School, at first in the old Oddfellows Hall, attached to the Red Lion in the High Street, and from 1932 as the County Grammar school in new buildings in Tuesley Lane which now house the sixth form college. 'Branksome' in Filmer Grove was for a time used as a preparatory school for boys, some of whom went on to Charterhouse,

Godalming Schools

ABOVE: BRANKSOME SCHOOL 1906 57058

This very substantial bargate stone building - five storeys and a basement - was originally a private house, but became a prep school known as Silvesters, the headmaster's name. Acquired by the Borough and used as offices (gas masks and ration books were collected from here in the war), it was transferred to the regional water authority when local government was reorganised in 1974.

RIGHT: THE INSTITUTE 1906 54691

The Farncombe Technical Institute was built in 1896. It held about 150 pupils, under five teachers. There was a carpentry room, a plumbing room, and five other classrooms. Tuition cost about £8 a term by 1928. Latterly it has been part of the Adult Education Institute, but was recently converted into apartments.

close by. St Hilary's girls' school was based on an earlier school, also in Tuesley Lane. It began with a handful of children in 1927 and now accommodates nearly 400. The Technical Institute, built in 1896, was also fee-paying, reflecting a growing awareness of the value of well-trained entrants to industry. One of the trades taught from the beginning was plumbing - the town having very recently had its first piped water supply installed.

No account of schools in Godalming can sensibly omit Charterhouse, built on the hilltop to the north of the town in 1872, though as one of the country's major public schools it has always been somewhat separate. Established in London 250 years earlier, it was finding surrounding development was becoming too constricting. The then headmaster, William Haig-Brown, was a man of vision who accepted the need for removal out of London, and had the tact and powers of persuasion necessary to overcome all the difficulties in the way. The move was beneficial to the school - numbers rose from 200

Godalming Schools

to 500 in Haig-Brown's time - but it was also of great benefit to the town. Gertrude Jekyll, in her book 'Old West Surrey', commented that 'Godalming was a very quiet, sleepy little town, from the time when coaching was killed by the railways…. The building of the Charterhouse School, finished in 1872, did much to awaken it, and to raise the value of land in the immediate neighbourhood…'. The Borough Council, composed largely of local tradespeople, were quick to see the importance of establishing good communications with the school, and built the Borough Road and Borough Bridge to ensure this. Another road which was developed following the building of the school was Peperharow Road. From little more than a farm track in 1870, by the end of the century it was, as the main route to the school, a properly made road with many houses for teachers and other staff. Friths were well aware of the potential for the sale of postcards of the school, and produced a good number.

Godalming Schools

Godalming Schools

Boarden Bridge 1906
54687

Until Charterhouse came to Godalming the only river crossing at the west end of the town was the wooden footbridge seen here - the 'boarden' bridge. To improve communications, the borough council built a road and the brick bridge next to the footbridge. The arches are high enough to allow boats to pass under, but since the water is far too shallow for boats people called it the 'Lunatic Bridge'.

Godalming Schools

Above: The View from Frith Hill 1898 41788

In its early years the main entrance to Charterhouse was along Peperharow Road, seen here from the water tower on Frith Hill. Development with houses for staff was rapid. Now there is not a single vacant plot.

Right: Peperharow Road 1907 57621

This view shows the substantial Victorian houses lining Peperharow Road. Note the water tower on the skyline, centre. Water was pumped up from the valley below; this facilitated the development of Frith Hill.

Right: Charterhouse 1927 79358

Built to a design by Sir Giles Gilbert Scott, the Chapel was started in 1922 as a memorial to the Carthusians who died in the First World War. It was dedicated in 1927, just after this photo was taken. After 1945, the memorial was extended to include those who died in the Second World War.

Godalming Schools

ABOVE: CHARTERHOUSE BRIDGE AND THE HINDHEAD ROAD 1906 57053

Built to link the school with some of the boys' houses in what was then Hindhead View Road, the early bridge became unsafe and had to be replaced. Contracting the road name to Hindhead Road led to confusion, as it goes nowhere near Hindhead, so it was renamed again, as Frith Hill Road. The bridge spans Charterhouse Road - itself renamed from Sandy Lane.

LEFT: CHARTERHOUSE, SAUNDERITES AND GOWNBOYS C1955 G23017

The statue in the foreground is of Thomas Sutton, founder of Charterhouse. In 1940 a German bomb fell in the open area, Founder's Court, blowing out all the windows but doing no serious structural damage.

FARNCOMBE

ABOVE: FARNCOMBE, HIGH STREET 1905 53233

Barely visible in the distance are the level crossing and signal box. There has been change here, with development on both sides of the road, though the white building in the centre and the terrace of houses remain. In the branch of Gammons, the tailors and outfitters, Jack Phillips, who was chief wireless telegraphist on the 'Titanic', was born in 1887. He earned more than local fame when he stayed at his post, transmitting the new 'SOS' signal until the ship sank.

BELOW: FARNCOMBE, ST JOHN'S STREET 1905 53231

The buildings in this photo are virtually unaltered today. M Barkway's shop on the left is still a shop: the back room was then used as a barber's, and still is. Reckitts Blue, advertised by an enamelled sign, was a whitener for laundry. Note the sign 'Teas' - the area was a favourite for cyclists' outings in Edwardian days.

Farncombe

FARNCOMBE, HIGH STREET 1905 53234

In 1905 Farncombe Street was like a village street, with shops and houses intermingled - there are bean sticks behind the wall, in the centre. It retains much of this character - the butcher's shop and the newsagent's are still shops. The Duke of Wellington pub, however, was recently replaced by a small housing developoment.

The name of Farncombe means the settlement in the fern valley. For centuries it was little more than a hamlet. At the time of the Domesday survey, there were 11 peasant families - probably less than 50 persons - and much of it was wholly undeveloped even 150 years or so ago.

There was, however, steady growth from about 1800, and by 1841 there were 173 houses with 804 inhabitants. After an abortive attempt to provide a separate church for the area in 1838, a second attempt a few years later was successful and the church of St John the Evangelist was built. Although the building was largely completed in 1847, costs had exceeded estimates and there were still debts to be cleared before it could be consecrated by the bishop. This was not achieved until 1849. Farncombe was then made a separate ecclesiastical parish. The population continued to grow, and in 1892 the civil parish was included in the Borough of Godalming for local government purposes.

'Although throughout the greater part of its history Farncombe has been overshadowed by, and to a great extent dependent upon, the neighbouring town that eventually absorbed it', wrote Dr J F Nicholls in his 1949 history of Farncombe, 'it would be entirely wrong to suggest that Farncombe was a mere appanage… of Godalming. It most emphatically has an individual character of its own; it is a real community …'. Something of that character shows through in Frith's photos, in particular those of High Street and St John's Street.

GODALMING
FARNCOMBE

FARNCOMBE

Farncombe, Catteshall Coffee Tavern 1905 53236

When this photo was taken, beer and spirits were cheap, and drunkenness commonplace. The Temperance movement was a reaction. This Coffee Tavern enabled working men to pass an evening without the temptation of alcohol. Beyond it can be seen a garage and cycleworks, almost at the end of the town - a fitting place to end this book.

Names of Pre-Publication Buyers

The following people have kindly supported this book by purchasing limited edition copies prior to publication.

Dennis & Helen Amy, Busbridge, Godalming

To my Daddy, Alan Bebbington, love Jessica

Karen (née French) & Kenneth M Bryant

The Budden Family, Godalming

Mrs Margeret Burgess, Godalming, Surrey

In memory of William Busby of Godalming

Harold Arthur Cole

Mick & Sue Company, Farncombe

Mr B A & Mrs D V Dance, Godalming

Mrs Daphne Darking

In memory of all the Darking Family

Mrs Pamela Darking

Mr Philip A Davies, Godalming

J R Dawson

Martin & Joyce Dennison, Godalming

Gordon Devereux, Godalming, 65th Birthday

Sean Dillon & Family, Godalming

The Drugan Family, Godalming

Win Elliott, 26th June 1911

D M Elson, formerly D M Staniforth, Farncombe

To Eluned in memory of Mum, with love, Dad

The Frenches, Beith, In Memory of Bob & Les

Paul Gamble, Godalming

Councillor R A Gordon-Smith, Mark Way, Godalming

Mr J H Gosling & Mrs P A L Gosling, Farncombe

Joe & June Greener of Godalming

For Georgina, Lucinda & Charles Haigh-Monk

David & Susan Hanna, Godalming

Mrs June Hatcher, Farncombe

B R Holden, Godalming

Keith Holland

In loving memory of Frances Hudson

J F Keefe, E M Keefe (Stagg), Farncombe

Peter, Christine & Simon Knottley

Mr & Mrs H W Lamble of Godalming

Helena Lawrence, Godalming

Ian & Kim Lawrence, Godalming

Jonathan Lawrence, Godalming

Samantha Lawrence, Godalming

Ruth & Timothy Lewis

Mr B D Lloyd

Mr H & Mrs B Lloyd, Farncombe

Brenda Marshall, Godalming

Past, Present, Future, Cyril & Sandy Netley

To the memory of Madeline Newell, Witley

The Overton Family, Godalming, Surrey

To Oscar Owen, Happy Birthday, love Mum x

Dr M & Mrs J Parry & Family

The Raggett Family of Ockford Ridge

To Judith Reading from Carolyn & Clive

In memory of Peter J Roberts, Godalming

Mrs Barbara Shenton (née Raggett) and son Peter

E C Siggery

Leslie Squelch, Adam Squelch, Godalming

Jennie Steele, 3rd June 1911

Mrs B S Steer

Mr David Steer

Mr John Steer

In memory of Angela Sykes 1942-2003

Christopher Ronald Sykes, Godalming

Kevin Paul Sykes & Neil Antony Sykes

Mr B A Taylor & Mrs S R Taylor, Godalming

L G Terry, Godalming

Val & John Theobald, Busbridge

Mr G L Tickner, Farncombe

Mr & Mrs K M Tickner, Guildford

Welcome to my parents, Joan & Reg Ward

Anne Weeks, Godalming

In memory of Chris Whitehead, Godalming

Mum & Dad, The Woodleys of Farncombe

Zoe & Gianluca

Index

Boarden Bridge..................................78-79

Boating on the River Wey......................54-55

Branksome Church....................................76

Bridge Street......................................48-49

The British Schools.............................74-75

Busbridge Church................................72-73

The Car Park..32

Catteshall Lock...................................50-51

Charterhouse..80

Charterhouse Bridge and the
 Hindhead Road..................................81

Charterhouse, Saunderites and Gownboys......81

Church Street....................................36-37

The Congregational Church........................72

Constitutional Club.............................42-43

Crown Pits..44-45

The Flour Mill...................................68-69

High Street.......14-15, 16-17, 18-19, 20-21, 22-23, 24-25, 26-27, 28-29, 30-31, 54, 56-57

Holloway Hill....................................32-33

The Institute.....................................76-77

Leroy's Boathouse...............................52-53

The Market House....................10-11, 12-13

Meath Home......................................38-39

Mill Lane...66-67

Municipal Buildings.............................46-47

The Old Forge, Pound Lane.......................65

The Parish Church..............................70-71

Peperharow Road................................80-81

Pullman's Mill..65

Queen Street....................................40-41

The Railway Station............................60-61

River Wey Camping Ground......................52

The Roman Catholic Church......................72

Town End Street.................................44-45

The Town from New Way.......................64-65

The Wesleyan Church and School................73

The White Hart..............................58-59,

View from Frith Hill................................80

FARNCOMBE

High Street......................................82-83

St John's Street.....................................82

Cattleshall Coffee Tavern......................84-85

FRITH PRODUCTS & SERVICES

Francis Frith would doubtless be pleased to know that the pioneering publishing venture he started in 1860 still continues today. Over a hundred and forty years later, The Francis Frith Collection continues in the same innovative tradition and is now one of the foremost publishers of vintage photographs in the world. Some of the current activities include:

INTERIOR DECORATION

Today Frith's photographs can be seen framed and as giant wall murals in thousands of pubs, restaurants, hotels, banks, retail stores and other public buildings throughout the country. In every case they enhance the unique local atmosphere of the places they depict and provide reminders of gentler days in an increasingly busy and frenetic world.

PRODUCT PROMOTIONS

Frith products are used by many major companies to promote the sales of their own products or to reinforce their own history and heritage. Frith promotions have been used by Hovis bread, Courage beers, Scots Porage Oats, Colman's mustard, Cadbury's foods, Mellow Birds coffee, Dunhill pipe tobacco, Guinness, and Bulmer's Cider.

GENEALOGY AND FAMILY HISTORY

As the interest in family history and roots grows world-wide, more and more people are turning to Frith's photographs of Great Britain for images of the towns, villages and streets where their ancestors lived; and, of course, photographs of the churches and chapels where their ancestors were christened, married and buried are an essential part of every genealogy tree and family album.

FRITH PRODUCTS

All Frith photographs are available Framed or just as Mounted Prints and unmounted versions. These may be ordered from the address below. Other products available are - Calendars, Jigsaws, Canvas Prints, Mugs, Tea Towels, Tableware and local and prestige books.

THE INTERNET

Over several hundred thousand Frith photographs can be viewed and purchased on the internet through the Frith websites!

For more detailed information on Frith products, look at
www.francisfrith.com

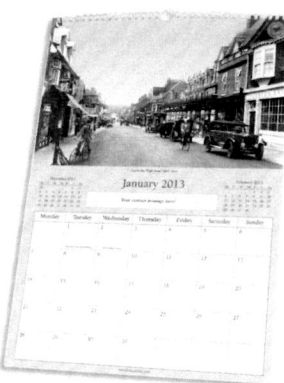

See the complete list of Frith Books at: www.francisfrith.com
This web site is regularly updated with the latest list of publications from The Francis Frith Collection. If you wish to buy books relating to another part of the country that your local bookshop does not stock, you may purchase on-line.

For further information, trade, or author enquiries please contact us at the address below:
The Francis Frith Collection, Unit 19 Kingsmead Business Park, Gillingham, Dorset SP8 5FB.
Tel: +44 (0)1722 716 376   Email: sales@francisfrith.co.uk

See Frith products on the internet at www.francisfrith.com

FREE PRINT OF YOUR CHOICE
CHOOSE A PHOTOGRAPH FROM THIS BOOK
+ POSTAGE

Mounted Print
Overall size 14 x 11 inches (355 x 280mm)

TO RECEIVE YOUR FREE PRINT

Choose any Frith photograph in this book

Simply complete the Voucher opposite and return it with your payment (to cover postage and handling) and we will print the photograph of your choice in SEPIA (size 11 x 8 inches) and supply it in a cream mount ready to frame (overall size 14 x 11 inches).

Order additional Mounted Prints at HALF PRICE - £19.00 each (normally £38.00)

If you would like to order more Frith prints from this book, possibly as gifts for friends and family, you can buy them at half price (with no additional postage costs).

Have your Mounted Prints framed

For an extra £20.00 per print you can have your mounted print(s) framed in an elegant polished wood and gilt moulding, overall size 16 x 13 inches (no additional postage required).

IMPORTANT!

❶ Please note: aerial photographs and photographs with a reference number starting with a "Z" are not Frith photographs and cannot be supplied under this offer.

❷ Offer valid for delivery to one UK address only.

❸ These special prices are only available if you use this form to order. You must use the ORIGINAL VOUCHER on this page (no copies permitted). We can only despatch to one UK address.

❹ This offer cannot be combined with any other offer.

As a customer your name & address will be stored by Frith but not sold or rented to third parties. Your data will be used for the purpose of this promotion only.

Send completed Voucher form to:

**The Francis Frith Collection,
1 Chilmark Estate House, Chilmark,
Salisbury, Wiltshire SP3 5DU**

Voucher
for FREE and Reduced Price Frith Prints

Please do not photocopy this voucher. Only the original is valid, so please fill it in, cut it out and return it to us with your order.

Picture ref no	Page no	Qty	Mounted @ £19.00	Framed + £20.00	Total Cost £
		1	Free of charge*	£	£
			£19.00	£	£
			£19.00	£	£
			£19.00	£	£
			£19.00	£	£
			£19.00	£	£

*Please allow 28 days for delivery.
Offer available to one UK address only*

* Post & handling	£3.80
Total Order Cost	£

Title of this book ....

I enclose a cheque/postal order for £ ....
made payable to 'Heritage Resource Management Ltd'

OR please debit my Mastercard / Visa / Maestro card, details below

Card Number:

Issue No (Maestro only):   Valid from (Maestro):

Card Security Number: Expires:

Signature:

Name Mr/Mrs/Ms ....

Address ....

....

....

.... Postcode ....

Daytime Tel No ....

Email ....

Valid to 31/12/26

Free Print – see overleaf

Can you help us with information about any of the Frith photographs in this book?

We are gradually compiling an historical record for each of the photographs in the Frith archive. It is always fascinating to find out the names of the people shown in the pictures, as well as insights into the shops, buildings and other features depicted.

If you recognize anyone in the photographs in this book, or if you have information not already included in the author's caption, do let us know. We would love to hear from you, and will try to publish it in future books or articles.

An Invitation from The Francis Frith Collection to Share Your Memories

The 'Share Your Memories' feature of our website allows members of the public to add personal memories relating to the places featured in our photographs, or comment on others already added. Seeing a place from your past can rekindle forgotten or long held memories. Why not visit the website, find photographs of places you know well and add YOUR story for others to read and enjoy? We would love to hear from you!

www.francisfrith.com/memories

Our production team

Frith books are produced by a small dedicated team at offices near Salisbury. Most have worked with the Frith Collection for many years. All have in common one quality: they have a passion for the Frith Collection.

Frith Books and Gifts

We have a wide range of books and gifts available on our website utilising our photographic archive, many of which can be individually personalised.

www.francisfrith.com